My
Father's
Geography

Also by Michael S. Weaver

POETRY
Water Song, 1985

CHAPBOOK
some days it's a slow walk to evening, 1989

My Father's Geography

Michael S. Weaver

University of Pittsburgh Press

Pittsburgh • London

The publication of this book is supported by grants from the National
Endowment for the Arts in Washington, D.C., a Federal agency, and the
Pennsylvania Council on the Arts.

Published by the University of Pittsburgh Press, Pittsburgh, Pa. 15260
Copyright © 1992, Michael S. Weaver
Eurospan, London
Manufactured in the United States of America

Library of Congress Cataloging-in-Publication Data

Weaver, Michael S., 1951–
    My father's geography / Michael S. Weaver.
        p.   cm.–(Pitt poetry series)
    ISBN 0–8229–3706–9 (cloth).–ISBN 0–8229–5469–9 (pbk.)
    I. Title. II. Series.
  PS3573.E1794M9 1992
  811'.54–dc20   91-50757
                                                                      CIP

A CIP catalogue record for this book is available from the British Library.

The author and publisher wish to express their grateful acknowledgment to
the following publications in which some of these poems first appeared:
Entropic Paradigm ("Switzerland"); *Gargoyle* ("Homecoming"); *Hanging
Loose* ("Luxembourg Garden"); *LIPS* ("The Washington Papers") and
Maryland Poetry Review ("My Father's Geography," "The Madman's First
Flight," "The Madman in Treatment").

"Back from the Arms of Big Mama" was first published in *Artist and
Influence* (Hatch-Billops Collection, Inc.).

"Atlantic City" and "The Picnic, an Homage to Civil Rights" were first
published in *Callaloo* vol. 7, no. 1 and vol. 12, no. 3. Reprinted by
permission of The Johns Hopkins University Press.

The following poems were first published in the chapbook *some days it's a
slow walk to evening* (Paradigm Press, 1989): "Ego," "Thanksgiving 1968,"
"Meditation for My Son," "Washington Papers, III," formerly "Archives,"
"The Missing Patriarch," "The Madman Raises the Dead," "The Madman
in Solitary," and "Tamo Before the Wall."

Let faithful love and constancy never leave you:
tie them round your neck,
write them on the tablet of your heart.

—Proverbs 3:2–3

Contents

Exploration and Writing the Way

Cartography and Dreaming

Ego

God's voice
is caught in
the crackling commotion
of thought,
like dried leaves—
breaking.

The Missing Patriarch

She peeked out from under
the old foot-powered sewing machine
a frightened cat, her eyes
still and aflame, her hair
darting about the iron curls
of the frame, her buttocks
filling the wide pedal, her daughters
twirling their fingers in their hair.
He pushed her there
when she accused him of loving
a schoolteacher, a light woman
of grace and power the men
eyed with scratching hands
from the wooden handles
of their ploughs. He slammed
her down until the wood
of the house set her marrow
to dancing and the waters
swallowed the shores that were her eyes.
He slammed her down
and strode out into the yard,
unmindful of the crisp fingers
of the sun poking his cheeks,
or the slow rustle of white sand
around his black shoes, deaf
to the dominant wail
of my grandmother behind him
or the screeching of my aunts and mother
like frenzied chicks beside her.

Beginnings

The house on Bentalou Street
had a cemetery behind it,
where the white hands of ghosts
rose like mist when God
tapped it with his silver cane.

There were giant pine trees
out front that snapped when
we hit them from the porch,
jumping like big squirrels
from the stone ledge.

Inside it had no end;
the stairs led to God's tongue;
the basement was the warm door
to the labyrinth of the Earth.
We lived on the rising chest of a star.

And on one still day,
I hammered a boy until
he bled and ran, the blood
like red licorice on my small hand.
The world became many houses,

all of them under siege.

Rough Riders on the Lawn

We sucked clover into our noses,
breathed it until the green flapped
like the tissue we held to the electric fan,
flipping over on our backs so the yellow light
forced our eyes shut. We chewed the grass
until it was milky and we felt like
we had consumed luck, we had protected
ourselves against the various legions
of winged reptiles who slept on edges
of dreams. The bell from the ice cream truck
came tinkling through the weeping willow;
we broke the lilies and low pine branches,
running to the banana split, leaving
the world in wreckage behind us.
On the steps, we retrieved dropped cherries
from the ants, wore the ice cream
around our mouths, forgetting luck,
forgetting the weakness of will.

The Picnic, an Homage to Civil Rights

We spread torn quilts and blankets,
mashing the grass under us until it was hard,
piled the baskets of steamed crabs
by the trees in columns that hid the trunk,
put our water coolers of soda pop
on the edges to mark the encampment,
like gypsies settling in for revelry
in a forest in Rumania or pioneers
blazing through the land of the Sioux,
the Apache, and the Arapaho, looking guardedly
over our perimeters for poachers
or the curious noses of fat women
ambling past on the backs of their shoes.
The sun crashed through the trees,
tumbling down and splattering in shadows
on the baseball diamond like mashed bananas.
We hunted for wild animals in the clumps
of forests, fried hot dogs until the odor
turned solid in our nostrils like wood.
We were in the park.

One uncle talked incessantly, because he knew
the universe; another was the griot
who stomped his foot in syncopation
to call the details from the base of his mind;
another was a cynic who doubted everything,
toasting everyone around with gin.
The patriarchal council mumbled on,
while the women took the evening to tune
their hearts to the slow air and buzzing flies,
to hold their hands out so angels could stand
in their palms and give dispensation,
as we played a rough game of softball
in the diamond with borrowed gloves,
singing Chuck Berry and Chubby Checker,

diving in long lines into the public pool,
throwing empty peanut shells to the lion,
buying cotton candy in the aviary
of the old mansion, laughing at monkeys,
running open-mouthed and full in the heat
until our smell was pungent and natural,
while the sun made our fathers and uncles
fall down in naps on their wives' laps, and
we frolicked like wealthy children on an English estate,
as reluctant laws and bloodied heads
tacked God's theses on wooden doors,
guaranteed the canopy of the firmament above us.

The Weekend Equestrian

In the yellow pickup,
I bounced out to your sixteen acres,
a boy narrow with the wonder
of Baltimore. Through
the cab window, I caught her smile
with the mole above her upper lip,
the bright way she corralled
your tales of Germany,
your hopes of raising Arabians
here outside a seaman's city,
where Black men grow pale,
waiting for dreams to
peek their sleek heads through,
after the grazing. I had
the brown saddle with me,
the one you left along with
a can of saddle soap and
instructions to raise the dirt
from the infinite curls in
the leather. I held it under me,
waiting for the fearful glide
of the horse, the apparition
of riding through the night,
through my father's dreams,
hoofs thudding the thunder
of words tumbling over words.

The Appaloosa

The one horse you gave me
you took back when she went insane,
when she began to chew wood
instead of the expensive grain
we bought from the feed store,
the grain that had the sweet smell
of molasses and was good for even
us to chew. She turned into
an ugly thing with her wild thoughts,
and I forgot about the beauty
expected of her when her blanket
filled out and complemented
her chestnut body and the name
the Nez Percé gave her. She rotted
and began to stink of promises
gone wrong, of gods avenging
their defilement. A man who knew
what to do with useless horses
came and took her away in
a wooden trailer she tried to chew,
and my tears welled up in huge drops
before they splattered on the ground,
as I trembled and realized I would have
to give up her own ghost for her,
ghost which she did not have, ghost
which she came here beautifully without.

The Dogs

You killed the Dalmatian puppy
with the wheel of your truck,
driving backwards over it until
the white with black spots popped
in the soft ooze of baby dog.
It was a simple and unexpected
flop of the wheel, and the children
cried, the children of the man
who owned the dog, the laziest farmer
in Woodstock, the man who let
pig shit collect until it was
three-feet thick and looked like
bad deviled eggs. The children
carried the dead puppy to ground
hallowed enough to wait for those spirits
who attend to the soulless, and
the truck spattered exhaust and oil
on the place where he left this earth,
as we drove off. In another year,
you killed another dog, this time
with the shotgun you ordered me
to bring to you, and I took his body
to the burn pile in a wheelbarrow,
watching how the flesh quivered
like the soft arm of your wife sleeping
in the yellow pickup, riding out
to where time is pregnant with surprise.

Homecoming

We inched into the night
at sixty miles an hour, following
the limitations of an AM radio,
a metal dashboard, cracking vinyl,
the constant flapping of the wind
on the windows like tongues
crowded along the margin of glass
and vibrating invisibly, leering
at your hair hot-combed to silkiness
and lacking only the fateful gardenia
or my caress. The population of men
played in my ear.

Not even the studied putrefaction onstage
with the rock idol waltzing through
on drugs, a senile composer traversing
the broken glass of failed notes
as silence fell to dust,
not even the loud but limp music
could unlock my eyes as you
betrayed my innocent approbation
and clung to the arms of athletes
and negotiators whose suits
hung on them like the bright tenor
or roses, not dull and unwilling
like mine.
                    "Hey boy, you want my phone number?"

No matter that I brought you here
and you left me, no matter
that I struggled to remember
a whole other song by a woman,
one who looked adoringly and sincerely
into my eye from the voyeurism

of television, no matter
that I knew in all my naivete
that I was naive and nothing
was of consequence as the world
expected nothing of me but
my attempt to consummate with you,
in one night, months of dreaming,
despite your indifference.

"It's the little man in the boat.
You don't know who he is,
you don't know nothing!"

Coming back to the circle of men,
breathless, I had to explain
how you eluded me, how your
nakedness blinded me as I ran,
lunging after you with hands
filled with an apocryphal music
and the weight of erections,
whispering to myself,
                "This is not the prize,"

patting the metal dashboard,
bellowing a dissonant love ballad,
meeting the spell of your breath,
wondering about the cymbal and brush
that is the cool temper and skin
of initiations and hunting,
the slick clicking of locks
in doors shutting in my face,
as refusal ran in rivulets
across your smile.

Thanksgiving 1968

I perched you like a hyacinth,
between my swaggering uncles
and the broken turkey browning,
steeped in a bubbling bath of gravy.

The men and the boys salivated
like strange sucklings when
I announced you were from Aruba,
beaten by the beaches in your hair.

I took the eyes of the young
and the old, the profligate tongue
of men who shared my blood,
my wish to tingle with your skin.

Night came in with rooted eyes;
I begged a ticket to the council of men,
a sad and silly novice ringer hoping
for the bell of your vulva under the wool.

Beneath us, the world careened and danced
to the fugue of firebrands and flags.

Bethlehem

I sat in a too-big plastic hat
on a metal corner by the shears,
watching the tin flash by
like a bright, liquid stream
that could decapitate or disembowel.

The mills are a gray city
that erupted and rose from Earth
like varicose veins, pores puffing
smoke into the thickened sky,
invading the world with its own metal.

Learning to believe the mutilation,
one man smacked and deprived of genitals,
another whistling as they sawed off his foot,
I accepted another kind of faith in work,
that of gin and eyes like cracked crystal.

I took a prodigal walk
from the university and manners,
following the horizon of my father,
treading on the prophecies and songs—
"Lord, child, don't trouble the waters"

The Washington Papers

I

I blow popcorn kernels
onto the mall,
after they prove basic
and irreducible like
the postcard evenings
of full trees and genteel
verandas on Capitol Hill.
With eyes closed,
I name each section
of the National Gallery,
making paintings anew,
studying the colors
in memory's hollow
hall. Joggers and kites
wake me in the last strokes
of a Flemish portrait.
I savor this moment
in splendid vision,
with the gray stone
behind me as motif,
where a carved heart
sings to heal itself.

II

Where everyone
comes
to organize and set
ideas in granite,
I came begging
to make
another life,

16

to set it smiling
in some
eternal woman.
Names and faces
escape me,
having multiplied
in the dream.

III

My father grabbed a plough
in the Smithsonian,
his first trip to a museum
and he could not believe
the waste of useful things,
empty reproduced rooms
where not even dust
inhabits the chairs.
A 1950s kitchen reminded him
too much of youth and love,
as he waddled quickly past.
Outside we walked
through the throng of pigeons,
not speaking.

IV

From your balcony,
we could see Virginia,
its verdant congregations,
with the city's pointed roofs
moving in the foreground

like priests. I held
my breath with my hands
to my stomach, as if
to slow time, to diminish
the universal duration
of the second so I
would never lose you.
Looking to Alexandria,
we shot black-and-white snapshots,
panning the city;
I slept on the naked glow
of your long neck flaming
in the door.

V

City of perfect accents,
city of antiquity,
of polished obelisks,
city of parthenons,
run by wet lips and silence—
come down from your arrogance,
enflame me, show me
the machinery of forgetting.

VI

Washington—
I will ease you
into nakedness,
part your hair
to let in the light,

slide your breasts
inside my cheeks,
travel your long legs
with my fingers,
slip your buttocks
in my palms,
kiss your head,
enter you,
claim loudly
the wet origin
of the word.

VII

Now when I walk
along Pennsylvania Avenue,
I hear doors shutting,
countless doors down
an endless hallway,
endings that were once
beginnings. My heartstring
is pulled with each slam.
I have
brought the final traces
of every woman
who ever left me to you,
under your downcast eyes,
crying and reclaiming.
Now I have another hope—
I will never weave this breath
into your collected tapestries,
never again wrench the heart.

Atlantic City

There is no one here with me
but a stranger from New Jersey,
separated by tons of water, weak caresses
of sand. A bigger wave sings from where
boats circle in the horizon's line, lifting
and dropping a lifeguard breaking against
the flow, we can hear and feel it now,
snatching our largest toes and flipping us
under. We hear and see and touch nothing but
wetness. On our feet again my wife screams
from the shore, throwing sand in the air to beckon,
the steel pier is beside me, beating the waves
back from her skirt, an old name in giant electric
blurting. The ocean's chest is low again, empty
of air and swimmers, we make our way back,
looking to be swallowed again, we have touched
a timeless point only to be cast on our feet, amazed,
robbed of the secret. We wade out again to be
part of the world's blood—I am no longer here,
the ocean laps the edge of the boardwalk at night,
my mother is in an all-white hotel by the grace
of her employer as a teenage nanny in Atlantic City.
Afraid to test the water, she holds the baby's hand
on shore, watching the beach littered with bathers,
water lurking out front all-knowing, all-seeing;
my wife trusts me here, leaving to collect shells.
The ocean is singing again, I wipe my mother from my eyes,
turn to feel it again, the sweep of my feet from me,
twirling head over heels, knees to my chin, twirling,
no earth, no heaven, no birth, no death, no recompense.
My wife pulls me from the foam and receding water,
piles her new shells on my chest one by one, laughing.
I can hear the song of eternity in them, roaring,
my wife piles her bag with shells and music.

The Madman's First Flight

I was in a church on New Year's Eve,
girding myself against the next year,
against the singing and explosions outside.
The minister showered us with words,
each one known only to God before he spoke.
Outside my shield shattered and fell;
I could hear every sound from mouths,
every crackling and thud from guns.

They were all words, people and things
became language, and I started to walk
on them, off the earth, slowly at first.

And then I flew above the world's noise
in its cage of glass to the eyes of the stars,
where not a thought could be touched.

The Madman Raises the Dead

The morticians have a way
of wrapping babies in plastic bags
where gases encase the bodies,
leaving no cuts or loud drainings.
But I washed you myself,
in sweet soap and warm water,
eased your tiny feet in white socks
and finished you with a blue top.

Now in an angel's loud armor,
I kneel near the stone cross above
your grave, watching the grass shudder,

waiting for this night to burn and fall
so that every dead soul that touches
your bones will fill with air and sing.

The Madman in Solitary

The clouds suggested themselves
beyond the mesh of screen and glass
as the persistent truth behind
the poker face of the quiet room,
with its blank walls and floor
designed with sickening swirls
that twisted my eyes until I screamed
at the gray nothing of being alone.

I clasped my naked skin
and scratched the day and time
on the mattress like some Copernicus.

A rogue had cracked and toppled my order,
swallowed a vital thread of my dreams;
I beat my pregnant head for the wise child.

The Madman in Treatment

On Thorazine constellations go
amuck inside my head, crack
and fly in silver specks against
the shivering liver walls of my brain.
Reason is a captive bull held fast
in a tiny capsule lost in thought.
I come back to the world
like flotsam floating to a beach.

Music barely matches the mad jazz
of bits of lives flying inside me.
There's a blue-hot fire in my soul.

My blood is Dionysian and wanton,
as I lie awake in the day, afraid of dreams.
There's a blue-hot fire in my soul.

Dialing for Dollars

After the "Dialing for Dollars Show,"
and the coffee and conversation
with neighbors who knew everything,
after the rituals and my mourning,
we headed down to the shopping center,
you driving the old black car,
the one we named like a dog we hoped
would one day run away, and in
the deadly mundane of the shops
and the Polish mothers who looked
just like you with their acrylic hats,
we stopped at the old wishing fountain
where I peeped sadly into the water,
weighed down by tranquilizers and fear
that I would never climb out of
this canyon of my own despair,
and you told another of your jokes,
like your favorite about the parrot,
not like the car but like a person,
a jive hip person that never faltered,
and you laughed until your dimples
twinkled under the fluorescent light,
poking me in my ribs to get me to smile,
and I grinned weakly, wanting to crawl
up inside your arms at twenty-four
and start all over again, back to
white shoes and formula milk and
fairy tales, away from this sense
that I had failed in everything,
even in being a just audience
to your comedy, to your tears.

My Father's First Baseball Game

You lumbered along the stadium
like a sinner being marshaled to baptism,
your head high and certain of convictions,
the busy chatter of the crowd beside you.

The radio is better, you declared,
and baseball is baseball regardless.
The wooden seat held you erect and mute,
glancing at the tiny figures in the field.

The open wealth of your first live game
came at you singly as the Negro Leagues
came up as you spoke of Satchel Paige,
Jackie Robinson and your ancient radio.

After the 9th, you fought the crowd,
fingering the ticket stubs in your shirt,
as we floated out into the night
with the deep river of white faces.

Meditation for My Son

When I go spinning,
your care is given
to the steel nerves
of reticent angels.

When I cannot hold,
my own heart drops away,
some sure finger from
a faded portrait follows
you in the thorn-filled
curves of man's road.

When I cannot dream,
I pray in blind rooms
that possible colors and bodies
will converge around you,
set you sailing over rocks,
away from the soulless.

When I am not whole,
I entrust you to seraphim
in their difficult dominion.

The Family Hymn

Grandma barked her infuriations
at my mother sitting below her mechanical
bed, clutching Grandma's dirty gown
from the night before and the bedsores,
crying softly into her hands, her head
a field of dried grass mad with the singing
of birds, and Grandma's fury forgot
the pardoning roll of spirituals.

In the kitchen as natural
as the soft easing of shadows
on the petals of her petunias out back,
my mother made my grandmother's lunch,
garnishing the tray with forgiveness
of days in White Plains where
she was her mother's knotty head convulsion,
and the trees wept with her,
as a child's pain is singular and sinful.

Up the stairs she hummed
"There Was a Time I Know,"
a family hymn I will pass on
to my daughters, a hymn that stayed
the monsters of illusion and anger,
as she turned the doorway to Grandma's smile,
which jumped from its place in the sun,
put its warm arms around my mother
and sang,
>   *"In the book of heaven,*
>   *an old account is standing*
>   *for sins yet unforgiven . . . "*

Back from the Arms of Big Mama

—an avuncular song for Alya Amani McNeill

In this room, in this chamber,
the sun stands like a woman
in an old cotton dress in August
shelling peas under maple shade.
In this room your great-grandmother,
Big Mama, slept away under the eyes
of the council of her daughters,
who kept a vigil, a deathwatch,
rocking back and forth in their chairs,
humming unexpected hymns,
huddling close together, making room
for the angels, seven feet tall
in blue pinstripe suits with silver
lights for eyes. Your great aunts waited
in this room where my mother
watched the door in the firmament
as these angels walked away with Big Mama.
Here my mother agreed to die.
And here I hold your entire body,
one month into the world,
brought here by my baby sister.
I show an old rough face
that has laughed and cried
with lips that want to pucker
against your candy cheeks.
I feel like a giant
suddenly discovering in his hands
the delicate and splendiferous
fragrance of the first breaths
ever taken by a tiny life,
my hands that have struck,
my hands that have caressed,
my hands that have pulled

against the hem of heaven.
I want to give all,
all that I own and may earn
so that you might have peace,
give all like St. Francis of Assisi
to lessen the pain and tears,
to make you go into the cavern
of this corpulent world
like Sojourner Truth, name
blazing against greed and lies.
I tell you your destiny
for which I am accountable,
tell you how you will grow
and shine brilliant among women,
attend Ivy League universities,
become a doctor when I am old
and desperately in need of one,
how you will not take
any of the shit men give to women,
how you will prosper and know
very little pain as now
the host of thousands
of minute soprano angels
who minister to the newborn
are here chanting a song
for children, something unpretentious
and familiar, like nothing I know.
Each time one of them
leans over to your beautiful ear
and says softly, invisibly,
"Alya, you are home, child,"
you smile and stretch and coo
in the arms of a big old uncle

with a scarred life who has come
through the spirit's wars
still hungry for your wise eyes
stepping forward from the light.

Navigation and Healing the Heart

Peeping Through Billows of Dust

At home in Baltimore, my parents spoke in a mixture of dictions, participating in varying grades of the southern speech they were born to and the more northern pronunciation of English that was official in this city where I was born, leaving me a person who feels distinctly northern. This self-image comes despite the many confrontations I have had with people who, upon learning that I am from Baltimore, resigned themselves to a picture of me as a southern gentleman. But my childhood is one of streets and alleys, of asphalt and concrete, of playgrounds and frozen courses for sleds, arising from my parents' southern roots admittedly. However, those southern roots were themselves offshoots of the genuine southern culture that lay below the Potomac, on the other side of Washington, D.C., a city some like to romantically call southern also, but one which is miles apart from the old capital of the south, Richmond, where both official and informal speech is of the south.

My mother embraced northern language and expression more quickly and thoroughly than my father. Sometimes in the afternoon, while she was in the midst of seasoning her chicken or "doing" the hair of a neighbor, my mother would get a call from Sears & Roebuck, where she did much of her ordering by phone. Her speech, which was more of the urban parlance most often referred to in the seventies as black English, became suddenly formal and a bit affected to my ears. I always found her manner with outsiders such as insurance people and store clerks as painfully stiff, but she enforced it with vigor, and was not always amused when my father wanted to reminisce about life in the country. He said he would like to be buried down there, but she would have none of it. So she rests today in a modern burial park with the markers that are flush to the ground and made of cast metal, nothing like the old family plots behind the community church in Virginia, just twelve miles from North Carolina, family plots where some kind member of the church comes occasionally to cut down the tall weeds that hide the crypts of my grandfather and grandmother.

With her five sisters gathered around her on the weekends, my mother would slip past that urban chic down-home to laugh and giggle as she and her sisters talked about growing up in Virginia, but for most of them it was only their childhoods they spent there. My grandfather died when they were young, and some of them had left even before then to come live with my grandmother's sister, who owned a beauty salon in a section of Baltimore called Turners Station. That was their way station on the way to becoming northerners. And during their weekend gatherings, often in my house where their mother lived for sixteen years, they recalled the old times, mostly the good because they loved laughter. They loved laughter, and, when they were young, they loved the excitement of being in the city and took to the task of being sophisticated much sooner than the men, who clung to a kind of chauvinism that was deeply entwined in southern being, a kind of tender but very male ego that expressed itself with the same gestures that cultivated fields and harvested crops down where you can get as high as a Georgia pine.

After working in the naval shipyards in Norfolk during World War II, my father came to the steel mills in Baltimore, where he remained for thirty-six years, making the forty-five minute ride to Sparrows Point, along a network of commuters where men had only to stand with their brown bags in their outstretched hands to hail a rider. Turners Station was very near to Sparrows Point. So my father courted my mother not far from where he worked. He came full of the gumption of being a young man and sat in my Great Aunt Margaret's living room, or, with permission, took her out for a short ride or walk, all the while supervised by my Aunt Margaret, a woman whose northern ways were deeply rooted. She and my grandmother were Goodes by birth, and the Goodes began the move northward in the nineteenth century, many of them settling in Pittsburgh, where my grandmother's cousin Mal

Goode, the journalist, graduated from the University of Pittsburgh in 1931. My father, who was fresh from the fields of Virginia and fiercely proud of his southern and rural character, obeyed Aunt Margaret without the slightest objection. He and my mother enjoyed their walks and rides, where she delighted in images of the city's glamour, while he took consolation in having work that paid more than following a mule and that allowed him to be close to the woman he wanted to marry.

My father did not make the concessions to northern ways that my mother did. His speech remains heavily southern, but, for all his dogged patriotism to the ways of the small farmer in the south, my father still does not retain the same accurate ring of speech that his brother Isaac had. Uncle Isaac never left Virginia for any extended stay anywhere above Washington, D.C., and when I saw the two of them side by side, I noticed how the roughly urbane movements of my father were different from his brother, who kept a slow, meditated movement like the sweet rising of air in the pines after a rain. My father has a little of the excitement of the city, mindful of how he keeps his shoes and just a little uncomfortable when that white Virginia sand coats them with a thin veil that makes him search for a cloth to restore the shine. My father may be a bit obvious in Harlem as being a bit "country," but he has lost that sure marrow that drives my relatives who remain in Virginia, most of them on my father's side.

So my home was this churning nexus where North and South, urban and rural, turned and beat against each other, wore each other down to their elements, and recombined in my life to be something I claim as northern. I saw the quintessence of my character as being hip, a tone my father looked at suspiciously, a tone my mother fought against arduously, and a tone my educators sought to forestall. Coming home from school was an interesting ritual, one whose importance I have heretofore overlooked. Seldom late, I opened the front door, when it was left unlocked, and proceeded to come into this churning mix, from which I was ushered every morning so that I might become a professional. The aroma of the food hit me as soon as I came in, but I was careful not to mess up the living room, which was kept in the same manner as the old sitting rooms in Virginia. I came in from a school system where the language was undeniably northern, where there was none of the southern undertone to be heard in the south where educators spoke in the drawl my teachers saw as incorrect. Moving inside the house, I passed through a chasm where I opened another soul, one that I did not bare in school, as I knew it was viewed there as unprogressive. I was indeed coming up in the world.

Normally I went to my room and changed my clothes before coming down to the kitchen where we all sat. My sisters and I took whatever seats were left after my father and mother took theirs, my father always at the head, and I have jokingly tried to enforce the old southern custom of making the eldest son next in the hierarchy at the table and elsewhere, but my sisters have always threatened me with bodily harm. But my father's rustic charm was the dominant mode at the table, as my mother, despite her hard-won urbanity, fell into the slow curves and quizzical pirouettes of speech I knew belonged in a more profound manner to my cousins whom I visited "down the country" in the summer, who watched our car peeping through billows of dust as it crept down the dirt road to my grandparents' house. As we ate in our kitchen there in Baltimore, in a neighborhood that was for many years the border between black and white, I watched my father and knew in some inarticulate cupboards of my soul that, although I ached to emulate him, the world would not let me be like my father.

A few years ago, my father told me how he once fought a hip city slicker who taunted him for being too "country," but my exposure to the quality of being hip was much more seductive. Hip came at me enticingly and then fled when I tried to touch it. The zone where hip appeared most distinctly for me was between home and school, as another ritual of extreme importance was presented to me, that of the way you walk, as in walk that walk and talk that talk. Young men signified themselves by the manner in which they walked. I still see the basic rhythm of this walk today in the youngsters and many of the older men, but it's rather naked without the adornment of accoutrements such as I was used to in the mid-sixties, namely the flat caps, the *creased* pants, the high collar shirts, the *polished* shoes, and the leather coats in winter, all of it worn on a delicate mobile of a body that hooked onto the air and tipped in synch with the unavailable secrets of time and culture, secrets that lie at the threshold between African and American. I envied this movement whenever I saw it, as my father never envied it, preferring instead the pure movements of his youth, relaxed—not possessed of the city's neurotic flips.

My schools fought against this northern manisfestation also. In grade school, I had loving, black teachers who took great pride in their professionalism and shunned what they saw as the hoodlum element. In junior and senior high school, my teachers, who were all white, fought the hip by just being who they were when they were unconscious, and by conscious manipulation when they were aware of the task before them. My senior high school touted itself as being the third-ranked public high school in the country, one where I marched the halls singing pep songs in German and wore a shirt and tie every day. I came home from this school to put in my four or five hours of daily studying, and my grandmother spoke from across the hall on her bed where she sat as an invalid, cautioning me not to study too hard because it might drive me crazy. It didn't drive me crazy. It drove me away from the hip, and I was never to be accepted therein, remaining more a certified square, full to the gills with the "correct" way of speaking and the "upwardly mobile" way of being in the world, all very definitely urban and northern in Baltimore, a major city in the growing megalopolis from Washington to Boston.

At least one fellow poet and friend has remarked to me that Baltimore has an old-world flavor, old world meaning European. I can see that in some of the older sections of the city, especially the downtown area near the Washington Monument, and it is a character I haven't seen in Richmond, Macon, Atlanta, or New Orleans, all of which I consider to be genuine southern cities, cities I think of when people refer to Baltimore as being southern, as they often unsuccessfully attempt to equate southern with backward. There is nothing backward about these southern cities. It's just that some of the people I've met in Philadelphia and New York are quite proud of their concrete rubble, and it's when I sense this attitude that I feel the comradeship with my father, although I know that, as someone born in Baltimore as opposed to having moved there, I have been given the northern character through the forces that helped to steer me through childhood and adolescence, a character that is adscititious to my father's way. What people perceive as the southern character in Baltimore is a quality of culture that I have seen all over Philadelphia, Newark, and New York. It is the presence of people like my father and mother, born and raised in the south to a certain age and then transplanted by the exigencies of economics. There is more south in the north than there is north in the south.

In intimate moments with my father, I am reminded of how far I am from the way of the small farmer in the south, although I have written about it. He will sometimes say or do something I don't understand or something I understood from my childhood and have forgotten. He reaches down deep into all of who he has been and has become to sound the language the way he did when he was a thirteen-year-old boy in Virginia in the mid-thirties, in the midst of the depression, when his baby brother played hooky from school by sleeping in the high grass, when he learned that you only send an old hound dog after a coon, when midwives and other knowledgeable women came to mothers in labor with curious brown bottles of medicine, when he learned to look at the sky and tell the world's moods and intentions, when his own father knew with increasing concern that there had to be an easier way for his children to live. My father comes out of all of this with a marvelous way of moving through the language, sculpting it as he goes, but still a distance away from that own genuine ring he himself had when he lived what he now remembers.

One day recently we were talking over the phone about a relative's health. I began by asking how was she. He answered slowly, saying, "Ah, she gittin back alright." I was bewildered, thinking she might have taken a turn for the worse, and I asked him what was it he just said. Clearly irritated, he cleared his throat and said slowly, "I said she doin alright!" That registered. After a visit with him, I have to be mindful of how long the good-byes take. He'll start in the kitchen or the bedroom by saying, "Alright." Then I wait through a few seconds of silence, as I know some part of him is still speaking. And he walks slowly to a point closer to me saying, "I'll walk you to the door," and the door soon becomes the back gate, and after twenty minutes we're driving down the alley, as I see him at the back gate, looking first to see how my tires are aligned as I go down the way, and then looking to those things growing in his backyard, green plants and grass that wave above the soil he knows is the anchor to his past. I watch him in the rear view mirror, as he moves through the old world.

An Improbable Mecca

I am here in the house
of my childhood, my youth,
of the quiet and whisperings
from walls that have watched
me lose my two front teeth
to a cousin slinging a baby doll,
walls that have recorded
the saltatory eruptions
in the living room floor
where the whole of us learned
the premeditated Manhattan
and the snap and flare
of the *Bossa* Nova, the Twist,
here in this house where quiet
ruled like an avenging saint
even when I rolled, drunk and dirty,
in the living room at seventeen,
home from college with hoodlum friends,
in the year of the Black Quartet.
This house opens its eyes,
reaches to me with hands held
together in silent prayer,
begging me to take every lesson
and go on with life peacefully,
out of its contemplation,
out of the lives it has absorbed,
out of my father's pondering step,
coming home in the evenings
in his brown, leather bomber jacket,
ecclesiastical and provident,
out of my mother's discordant
singing as she put yellow ribbons
in my invalid grandmother's hair,
singing old spirituals being quickly
removed from new hymn books,

always falling back to her favorite,
"Pass Me Not, O Gentle Savior."
Her humble cry resounds
in the tiny mind of my ear
when I slide my hands down the walls
as I ease down the stairs of
this house where mother and grandmother
died, where the bones of this home
screamed until they were thin
as glass when I lost my mind.
This house throws back its head
and laughs in a resplendent roar
that goes up in bubbling clusters
when I ask it to remember
the first poem I wrote at eight,
the Sears & Roebuck bicycle
with whitewalls and headlights,
the first girlfriend in the fourth grade,
the first wife at nineteen,
the long hours of studying,
the lectures on ancestry from Grandma,
the delicate cloth of talking
and sharing I built with my father
as we became the next two
on the prophetic end of the pew,
the anxious, sleepless nights
while we listened to Bessie
frying the chicken for the trip
down-home, south to Virginia,
back to the embracing roots
that made us believe unfalteringly
that we were truly wealthy,
the pious Sunday mornings
when I marched off

to the Baptist church quiet and measured
like the Methodists and Lutherans,
with my usher's badge and my belief.
This house stands before me
and in my memory, a monument
perfectly aligned to the stars,
luminescent and sentient,
a life in and of itself and ourselves,
as patient and kind and suffering
as anyone could ever hope a house
to be when chattering children
kick in its lap, men lie in it,
trying to accommodate their future,
when women paint it with song
from the old world of patriarchal law,
when death comes lusting after it
with sledgehammers and stillness—
I come to the front steps
and sit as I did when I was a child
and hope that I can hold to this
through life's celebrations and calamities,
until I go shooting back
into the darkness of my origin
in some invisible speck
in an indeterminable brick
of this house, this remembering.

The Message on Cape Cod

We have slept in
the wide electric arms
of love. At noon we pass
a wedding of celebrities,
count the limousines
as we stalk the souvenir shops.
An invisible and peculiar wire
holds this life together,
and we cling to a molecule
proudly. In the restaurant
we chant a child's lullaby
over the clam chowder,
and you remember another
tune and still another
until the light dims
in the eye of the baked fish,
and the waitress retires
to her stool, wrapped in smiles.
We move down the beach
in the evening, always
one failing step ahead
of the March wind, looking
out on the vast tongue
of the ocean to where
whales passed. A sweep
of the fog light circles around;
the smug authority of the water
allows us a sudden privacy,
and we make love behind
a giant log washed to softness.
A boat eases past, investigating,
and, dressing, we ease back
to the wooden stairs of the cliff,
counting the eyes that see.

Taking Our Son to MOMA

We saw Frank Stella in wet snow and cold,
moving down the street in a giant mass,
you with your private giggling and snowballs,
he with his premature size and hormones.
Up against the wall in the museum,
he almost touched a spike projected by Stella,
a small tower bursting from the painting;
I whispered, "We cannot press flesh to the priceless."
To the pizza parlor on Seventh Avenue,
he looked for puddles to wet his feet,
an old habit from a previous life where
he was a missionary in a tropical rain forest,
or a seaman. Riding to Chinatown, the faces
hovering in lit signs grabbed for our eyes.

The Honeymoon

The saleswomen
blessed us with hints
of jealousy, turning
the corners of the plastic
bag until the veins
rippled and showed
the quick route
of their blood.
Around the corner
their dark eyes followed
above the window displays,
becoming hard pebbles
that glared and raged loudly
along the empty boardwalk.
You broke one of the ceramic
goblets on a stone,
cutting your calf
with a slow dribble in the sand.
I pressed your leg
with two tight fingers
until the blood dried,
and we picked the broken pieces
from the sand, chatting
on about glue until we could laugh,
until we could walk in the sand,
not thinking of sinking.

Maple Mountain

In the low lip of the mountain,
fresh undergrowth and soft soil
like the delicate flesh of a mouth
extends from some great head

like Nat Turner's or Solomon's,
here we begin the climb, you
swatting innocent maple leaves
where plastic tunnels small as pencils

connect from trunk to trunk,
down to the gray syrup store
on the highway. Somewhere
away from us, black bears tear

apart the tiny veins of leaves,
kicking their feet over their heads,
tumbling in the sunlight,
their hair as sharp and brilliant

as the consuming wall of sleep,
and they rumble through the mountain's
magnificent head to remain aloof,
unseen while I position a timid shoe

weakly in the rocks as we leave
the lower lip and put our tiny hands
in the nose of the giant,
imagining how the top of this head

must be, what intelligence
is fed to it from the sky,
in this intimacy with heaven.
In the cliffs I grow insistent,

and you struggle from below,
peeping to keep me in sight.
I nearly stumble and break a twig,
remembering that I have a child,

someone following me, examining
my shadows and created history,
looking for beacons along the trail
that shoots us back to God.

We trade riddles and I introduce you
to the Greeks, explaining the duty
of teacher to student as
the peak comes in sight, knowing deeper

that teacher is father and flesh,
as the sky rolls over the top,
promising the plateau that is
both beginning and end of mountain.

Looking down we see how to jump
from there to any point in the world
circling beneath us, two minds,
two hearts, two steel chords against fear.

Tiny dots of people
cross over to the syrup store,
fathers with their sucklings who
kick in the gravel, blink at the sun.

The Helper

Floating in your flannel gown you sit
with a book propped up on an invention
the sheriff made, sipping your coffee
and breaking the hard toast on the edge
of your mouth, careful not to pressure
the front of your smile, the weakest
point. Your small head intently
consuming the book makes me think
of a Yeshiva, only this is a New England novel,
where something ingenious happens on
a dull farm owned by the rich and uninventive.
We exchange our good mornings and your eyes dance
to thunderous workings of infinite strings
in your head that dare not break
for there is where your mettle is kept
to this side of the world, to a mission.
I amble to the stove for my own coffee,
catch a snake changing his resting place,
going against gravity again,
moving to another corner of the woodpile,
and I smile to remember that
I am perhaps not so urban, perhaps
I am home here in the mountains,
on your farm of rocks, that
I am used to the roughness
you call Yankee courage, the kind
of spirit that let you run
down the White Mountains like the snake,
full speed in the opposite direction,
something men use drawing boards and machines
to accomplish. Your white hair
is still beside the colonial fireplace
and the Shaker furniture. I catch
the stately nose of the doe
moving across the lawn. With my feet

stretched to the cold, stone hearth,
kicking the ashes under my shoes,
I wonder how I managed to grasp
my untenured life and lead it here
to this perfect composition, you
gracefully swinging at the end of life,
throwing me a line—

"Come on, young man. Take hold."

Tamo Before the Wall

After the first thousand days,
fractures running like nameless lovers
go full and vibrant in the afternoon,
tall women dancing down
from clouds with trails of lace.
He tips his ear to invisible sobs
working in gray indentations,
a woman's protestation or her grief--
he shudders in his faded robe,
his ears no longer tuned to a woman's voice.
It was spring inside a house
where the colors rippled under
the curtains twirling; she brought him
his cooked meat and a prophecy
on a tray painted with gold birds.
They made love past the hour of the cock.
Now he clings to his body and the wall,
with one silk nerve cast in silence.

Exploration and Writing the Way

My Father's Geography

I was parading the côte d'Azur,
hopping the short trains from Nice to Cannes,
following the maze of streets in Monte Carlo
to the hill that overlooks the ville.
A woman fed me pâté in the afternoon,
calling from her stall to offer me more.
At breakfast I talked in French with an old man
about what he loved about America—the Kennedys.

On the beaches I walked and watched
topless women sunbathe and swim,
loving both home and being so far from it.

At a phone looking to Africa over the Mediterranean,
I called my father, and, missing me, he said,
"You almost home boy. Go on cross that sea!"

Canadian Awe

At the tollbooth the officer
did not give me time to try
my high school French, moving on
quickly to English, assured of
my inability to deal in the tongue.
We laughed with each other because
this was the right love, the one
to end all our efforts in the past,
the one to cure the need to be constantly
assured that someone is near. Away
from the booth, we passed the shop
where earlier I had come with my son
and bought him a penknife to bring
out the smile from that worried
mouth, afraid of what the distance
between us was doing to father and son.
We drove on around the curve
of the highway where Canada looks
distinctly different from America,
where you feel that you are foreign
to this country and it is foreign
to you, which is the awful truth
before love and after love's death.
In the hotel you pressed me for some
guarantee of what I felt, and I gave
until inside me an unknown ache
came to live, as I forgot all the women,
even the yellow face of the mother
of my son.

Luxembourg Garden

I am set off
from men and women
by their tongues,
my brown-red skin,
their words I hear,
but am only learning
to speak, by a music
I am listening to,
for understanding. Nature
has caught me here,
in trees, sections
of grass, neatly laid
rows of plants. I have
been freed by language
to think how much there
is in the eye of a pigeon
that looks like me, black
and ploughing through
a thousand pat assumptions.
I set my croissants down
beside me, cover the juice
to keep out the leaves.
Thousands and thousands,
a universe of nerves
are placed on my every move—
from the leaves in trees,
from the blades of grass,
from the squirrels holding
me at bay. I am coming
to an early peace, the one
given when everything
familiar is taken away.
We see the plan of life.

This bench is on earth
owned once by the Medicis.
I watch the police in
their crisp blue, guarding
the grass. Nothing matters.

By the Seine

The mist of the sky's mouth
hovered over the roof of the Louvre;
an old painter on spindly legs
walked her patient mongrel to the Seine;
the banner of the Dubuffet exhibit
draped the long perspective of shutters
from old houses kneeling on mended knees;
flat boats lay tied to the banks,
black and square in lacquered quiet;
the Île de la Cité shot its cheeks
out broad and determined,
the original mother in stone;
I gazed in the eyes of the window
for keys to the rapid turning
of this tongue that coats the teeth,
that seduces with chocolate and cheese;
I looked at the dumb point
of my pen, angered by its impotence
and my starved wish to bring you
the hurried frames of a city
whose life was flashing in my hand,
filling the stations of empty dreams.

Cannes

The grove of naked swimmers is behind me,
women with their breasts tapping their chests,
melting into the white glare of the beach;
a stilted wind tucks the leaf of a palm tree,
lets it fly until it flaps softly over a cloud;
the hundred crazy stripes of the umbrellas
are like the eruption of gay pimples in sand;
old couples in white go past me chattering,
pointing to the villas set on their haunches,
with their broad noses pointing to the sea;
cabs dart past the windows of specialty shops,
where young women search for famous actors;
tops of yachts and sailboats are laid to the sky,
like the variegated patterns of a lily field;
God's breath excites the tingling smiles in sunglasses;
my bag of croissants jingles against my thigh,
I lift my camera to my eye, pan the shore.

Switzerland

Night settled
with the little Texan
nestled above me,
comparing the ice caps
to shopping centers and cows.
I stared out the window,
looking for the spots
of lights from the towns,
clusters of white pinheads
suspended in the valley.
The huge thighs of the mountains
thickened the darkness,
huddled together like fat dancers
with hair of ice and snow,
the train tipping over
their toes.

An Evening in Madrid

Don Quixote is dwarfed
by the rolling shadows
of evening creeping over
the mountains; his little friend
sings his metal body
in the blackness. I stop
for ice cream, hungered
by the long trek to the Prado
and the young stares
of starched soldiers
pointing loaded machine guns.
Every tongue and mouth
around me snaps and beats
tiny cymbals I do not know.

A Café Window

They came at night in soft cotton suits
with the tiny Italian shoes with tassels,
turning the corner past the café with mouths
open wide to laughter and singing, following
the proud women who bring their African loves
out at night to whisk through the traffic,
tantalizing the gaping mouths of tourists
and the firm and folded arms of old women
in the doorways pointing and shaking fingers.
I wiped my mouth where the beer had formed
a lining of foam and rubbed my glass around
in circles on the table. One couple disappeared
and the cars whirred by and filled the emptiness.
I wondered what museum and what art was open
to the chic at night, what timeworn and honored
statue they were about to grace. The Parisian
stone turns a proud gray in the darkness,
putting a solid affirmation in a city that is gay
in the day, one that rivals the iris and the rose
in their frailty and splendor. The men at the bar
shifted from one tired foot to the other,
wobbled on buckling knees as the drinking wore on.
Another couple came, the head of a promenade
on their way to some point in the night,
African men and French women in intimate air.

Against the glass between us I lifted my hand
and blew a slow and silent kiss to their star.

New England

At night a voice
lends its enchantment,
and New England is owned
by the pondering dead.

Lovers in the Needles
As twilight set fire
to bobbing hills of snow,
making the tinkling reflections
in the crystals explode
in tiny, brilliant burstings,
she sat alone in the kitchen,
by the shaking window
rattling in the rough groove.
She sat knitting a nightshirt
for the child to come,
sighing for the tiny graves
in the grove of birch and elm,
reciting quietly the prayers
that set their young bodies
in the cold earth and snow.
She sat until she saw
a young sailor running up
the Boston Harbor in April,
mangoes stuffed in his coat,
gulls chasing round the masts
of brigs at the dock, and
he reached for her lips.
She felt flush, then hollow,
her lips pasted on glass;
she opened her eyes,
the snow overcame her again,
her hands fell in the silence
of wood popping and whistling
in the hearth, of shadows

without voice sliding
from wall to vicious wall,
only his militia certificate
and the old, impossible boots
that thrilled and appalled.
Her eyes shot out and around,
the moon had captured her,
full and beckoning,
over the flickering snow.
She put a leaf in the Gospels
and found the rope, marched
slow and weightless, singing
up the stairs, heavenward.
Her benediction came with
the squeaking yell of timber
burdened with her weight,
the swinging dress and collar,
her soft, white feet
pedaling the air above the stool,
her tongue jammed and caught,
as she tried to sing "Amen."

In colonial New England
women braved the winters
and died young. The coffers
were filled with Africans,
molasses, rum, and oil.

The Minister's Compass
Some Sundays when red maples bloom,
I sleep in the Baptist church
squatting in Old Providence's hill,
unbeknownst to the tours,
to old men in herringbone.

I step among them and search
their eyes for the gratitude
their fathers hoped for
as they slept in forecastles.
I look in slavering mouths
for the hallelujahs
to pump up when they think
of who packed the cobblestone,
who delivered the mackerel and cod,
who drifted down Africa's coast,
collecting the naked slaves,
who drummed God in their heads,
who gave the Cross to Indians,
who took this blessed nation
out of heaven's launch
and set her virgin hull
into the world's deep blood.
Stopping, I hear nothing
but cheap chatter of the moment,
and the very next moment,
no vision of the future,
only the indolent stare,
with tidy talk of television.

Moving among the living,
I think of how freedom
is a mandate for everyone,
how I have come to own nothing.
My heart is confused,
a compass on the spin.

Cherubs in the Glen
When the madam paced
the wharves in Boston,

she looked for something special,
a delightful, naked girl
who might have died on board
with greater cargo, but stared
now with pleading eyes,
and she became a Wheatley,
a genius like a warbling finch,
prodigious, gay, and fragile.
She took the breath away
from gaping strangers, turning
the language and fixing it
like someone adorning
a forest with Chinese silk,
pasting the red walls of the Veil
with the human constant.
When they buried
the four fallen from fighting
in the Boston Massacre,
she rushed to her quill
and penned a tribute.
Her heart was full
of song, and when it quit,
she fell dead with a child,
long after the brave lights
held in the Old North Church.
She fell dead with a child,
beyond the plea of Diana,
a woman in colonial New England,
　　　"To me the meanest flower that blows can give
　　　　　Thoughts that do often lie too deep for tears."
Her silver gleanings
were the songs in the elms
above the head of a ship caulker

once a slave who turned
the word again to kindle
the soul's soft string.

The Minister's Heart
From a sermon's midst,
I would catch you in the square,
dark hair flaming deep,
enchanting, a tune rising
from your head like a chorus.
Your soft, counted
movements under the trees
like the slow plucked
strings of a harp halted
my hand holding the quill
until I strode the room,
begging grace not to lift
its lace hem from my head,
begging for the very light
to leave my eyes so I could
take the world through my hands.
That only fed Satan's laughter,
for as I thought of the world,
I thought in an instant
of a frightened flock of finches,
and your hands, the nimble grasp
around the neck of a bottle,
or the assured laugh you gave
to the lies of the fishermen,
as your neck arched white
in the sun, turning a hundred shades
as you walked. I ached
and wept like a green sailor,
pouring my tears on the pages

of the Psalms, banging
Proverbs with a clenched fist.
I stripped to the waist,
beat myself with tight leather
to loosen the domination
of the flesh, but each time
I shamefully touched myself,
it was you my soul cried for,
you my very being denied grace for,
you I wanted to wrap
in the black leaves of my coat
and press through my naked breast.

Now I have you,
my fingers hold that hair
that derives its power
from the trills of the moon.
At night I pull the cloth back
for the stars to shine
on your filling breasts,
the soft rising of your belly,
to set miniature twinkles
in the toes I paint
with my tongue in the morning.
I hold your head and
am not shaken by the spectre
of Lucifer dancing in the window,
the dance of poor Job,
for I have nothing but my life,
and that I would give
for you. In the mornings
when you bring the blueberries,
I hold your hand as long
as prudence will allow in the day,
before the serpent's head

rises in the pious eyes,
before God's rage goes shouting
in the woods, beating wildly
from tree to anchored tree,
and I am held to you
by the flame of breast on breast,
the sense of immortality
I feel when I gaze
on the crown of your thighs,
a white and auburn bloom
that rules me with its perfume,
that makes my self-flagellation
a mockery of love's florid dignity.

And do not die, never die—
for the Puritan councils
and our entangled exegesis,
I will wear the dread emblem
branded on the flesh of my heart
until it takes my breath,
and I sleep to the Day of Doom.

The Whalers
We were off island
for two weeks, headed
south for the leviathan.
I was on deck sleeping,
the sun burning pleasant
fires in all my pores,
when from the crow's nest,
"Blows. There she blows."
They trampled me,
running to starboard side,
"Get up you old nigger,

there's one of God's beasts
bathing above like
a ship overturned and hull up.
Get your one good hand
you lazy nigger, get it now."
The captain bellowed
to lower the boats,
the whale lounging in the sun,
resting from charting the world,
its great soul giving thanks
in sprays that shot up,
seen for miles around,
talking in thunderous bass
to all the Deep's populace,
issuing kingly demands,
while its death sped on
in cedar whale boats
with harpoons like razors
and whale lines set
to follow him to the floor.
When they cut him,
he sliced through the surface
as if he had wings,
taking both boats and crew
on a Nantucket sleigh ride,
breaking one, drowning the crew,
taking the other until
it could not budge a fluke,
and the final point
was cast in his eye,
a sin as sure as extinguishing stars,
for I heard him sing
when they did it,

when they cut his lungs
and the thick blood ran,
unsure of a world
it had lived in but never seen.
On board, rolling the blanket piece,
the clouds turned sorrowful faces
in their white juxtaposition,
the scorns of angels
watching a huge saint
undone to the bone,
its dignity boiling in the tryworks,
while I changed the sea water
beneath them with my good hand,
the bad one maimed by a whale
that sounded and took whale lines
and my hand with her,
the hemp burning me to the bone.
This one gave two hundred barrels,
and we plunged farther south,
farther than the Indians dreamed
when they hunted with canoes,
boiling the monarchs of the deep
on beaches in tryworks there.
We headed for the Pacific
and the giant flesh
that swam there in herds
governing the Earth
from Antarctica to the Arctic,
relentlessly hunted by men
afraid of earth oil
and disappearing profits.

And the old whalers on shore
lived comfortably sometimes,
after the storms,

the ships' bones bleaching
like the whales' in the sun.

Provincetown
Ambling through the cape,
we begin at Buzzard's Bay,
stopping in the full moon
to play with an itinerant retriever,
watching his wet body
melt in the trail of moonlight
linking the beach to the gods.
He loses the wood floating
and threatens to drown himself
with determination in the black water,
until we throw more flotsam,
and he yelps to celebrate
the deception, the call away
from the dead end of duty
that swallowed men
and made women suck and choke on
the delicate lace of loneliness.
Driving on, the wail of ocean
is hushed by the towering woods
until we reach the point,
the first landing of Puritans,
where Cook assembled his thespians
in Mary Vorse's old wharf,
looking out the window,
dreaming of some revival,
some Greek organic seed
to deify the American soul,
as O'Neill carved his dark emperor.
We watch for contented artists
who sign bloodless treaties with despair.

At night bright ships sail the sky,
pushed on by the songs of ghosts
given back by history's rituals
for an eternal voyage back to love.

Providence

In the car with our chicken and biscuits,
we came to the hushed roar
of Providence, the city of dead engines
and abandoned space being converted
to kitchens and family rooms;
the sun tucked us into the sharp angle
of the car turning off the highway
as we headed for some by-product
of the hypnotic water, the water
that beckons, that fills the linings
of your brain with a slow song
that calls you back again and again
to this unlikely plantation.

On the grass, against the tree,
wiping sweat while you focused the Nikon,
I thought of a night there on the hill
where the loneliness piled into my pores
like stone needles driven slowly,
of a snowstorm that made this city
of slowness stop and crawl into the past,
while I fell into a depression
that came from the heel of heaven,
appearing suddenly like a famine,
as I plodded through Brown,
the Brown of the old slave trader,
the Brown of the elite's children.

The camera clicked, pasting me
against the wall. I embraced the railing,
felt the flickering eyes of the dead.

About the Author

MICHAEL S. WEAVER was born in Baltimore, Maryland, in 1951. He received his B.A. from the University of the State of New York and his M.A. from Brown University. He has written and published fiction, and he has had two plays produced. In Baltimore Mr. Weaver worked as a warehouseman and a journalist. He has contributed essays to the *Philadelphia Inquirer* and the *Baltimore Evening Sun*. In 1985, Mr. Weaver was a National Endowment for the Arts fellow, and in 1989, he read for the Gertrude Clarke Whittall Fund of the Library of Congress. He has taught at Essex County College, Seton Hall University School of Law, the Borough of Manhattan Community College, Brooklyn College, and New York University. Currently, he is an assistant professor of English at Rutgers University, in Camden. He lives across the Delaware River in Philadelphia with his wife, Aissatou Mijiza, and his son, Kala Oboi.

Pitt Poetry Series

Ed Ochester, General Editor